Jealousy, Envy

Proverbs 14:30

"A calm undisturbed mind and heart are the life and health of the body, but envy, jealousy, and wrath are like rottenness of the bones."

This is a short study about how families and generations fall into the pits of jealousy, envy and strife better known as an ungodly dysfunctional family. How often does jealousy, envy and strife influence the family structure? It happens more often than we realize. We just look at it in diverse ways and assume it is what it is. What is it and where does it come from? We have all either experienced it in our own family, or seen it happen in other families. Toxic sibling relationships can result if parents are unavailable, depressed, aggressive, narcissistic, or controlling or favoring one child over the others. When the parents do not set boundaries or manage the siblings, relationship healthily. Although many would deny it, parents often favor one child over others. When they do so explicitly, the Golden Child and the Black Sheep Dynamic can result. The Outcast of the family is the scapegoat who is always portrayed as" bad" and can do nothing right. With the defense mechanism of projection and projective identification, the family projects all woes onto the scapegoat. The scapegoat is pushed aside most of the time and blamed when things go wrong.

As the parents think of the Golden child as an extension of themselves, the parents would not allow the Black Sheep to threaten the narrative they have set up. So, when the scapegoated child does something well, their achievements are ignored or dismissed. The Golden child always has to be the best in everything, and the Black Sheep can only be acknowledged to the extent where the Golden Child 's brilliance remains unthreatened.

If the Black Sheep has internalized their family's message for them, they may struggle with self-esteem, carry toxic shame, and do not believe they deserve to be happy and successful. Unconsciously, they may feel if they achieve something they will be attacked and criticized. So even as adults, they may sabotage to dodge the attack they unconsciously expect a sense of loneliness for the rest of their lives.

Being the Golden child, however, does not mean everything is perfect. "Quoted by Jung from an article in Psychology Today. The Golden child is the one parents project their aspirations onto.

Whilst the Odd one out "Black Sheep" is pushed to be self-controlling and not governed by outside forces and find their way in life, the Golden child is forced into enmeshment with their controlling parents. They are subtly punished or threatened if they do not follow the path laid down for them. Therefore, even as adults they always feel they must 'do the right thing' or appease their parents. They may struggle to be spontaneous or do something outside the conventional. Also, the Golden Child may suffer from unconscious guilt as they see their sibling being unfairly treated but could not do much about it. Later in life, they may have a rescuer complex' be attracted to vulnerable partners who need help or exhibit people pleasing behaviors and subjugation.

The mature One and the Eternal Child

The Mature One is in this sibling dynamic is the one who is mature beyond their age. They are always responsible, disciplined, and reasonable. The Eternal child, in contrast, is typically the opposite. They are the wayward ones who follow their own will, are driven by passion, and cannot discipline themselves. Jungian article in Psychology Today, The Eternal Child embodies the Puer/Puerlla archetype, a person who is forever young. They detest boundaries, limits, and commitments. They have a lot of ideas about what they can do in the future but rarely put the challenging work to make their dreams come true. They have little tolerance for hardships, so whenever things get hard, they escape into their fantasies. They may run from one situation to the next, one job to the next, one relationship to the next and never commit to any meaningful course of actions. They are fun to be with but are not dependable partners. In many ways, they are children living in grown up bodies and have difficulty being a functioning adult in the real world.

When there is an Eternal Child in the family, there is paradoxically the Mature One. Dynamically, the Mature One feels that since their sibling is a disappointment, they cannot afford to be.

Thus, they feel they have no choice but to follow the path that was laid down for them, and to become a successful functional member of society. The Mature One does everything that is expected of them. But this is not a free choice. They do so because absolute compliance is what was once required of them.

They may be filling in for a depressed parent who makes it clear they have no extra energy for parenting, or they are overcompensating for violent and unpredictable parents who would be enraged if things were less than perfect. They do not feel they are allowed to let their hair down, relax, have fun, and do something outside of what was expected of them. While they over function at home, they are also likely to over function at their work, in their romantic relationships, and in their parenting; eventually they are overburdened with responsibilities and may burn out.

One factor that makes this dynamic complicated, especially when it turns into adult sibling rivalry, is envy. For all their lives, the Mature One is consciously envious of how carefree their younger sibling seems to be. They love their siblings but could not help but feel bitter and resentful for the fact that they never had a real childhood. Caught in a bind between love and resentment, loyalty, and the need for freedom, the Mature One may be plunged on to an emotional and existential crisis in later life.

The Bully and the Silenced One

In a healthy scenario, a parent would discipline a child when they speak disrespectfully or act aggressively. Some parents, however, may fail to do so due to their attachment needs and trauma history. They deeply fear conflicts and abandonments do not do anything to discipline a child that is acting out. The parents' inability to assert parental authority means the children are left to find their limits, which is an impossible task. When there is sibling abuse, the polarized dynamic involves a Bully and their victim, the silenced lone. For the Bully, being able to get away with aggression and even abuse is not a blessing. Children need boundaries and often evaluate to find if there are any. When the Bully cannot find the lines that should have been drawn by their parents, the world would feel like a chaotic and frightening place. Often, the Bully is a neglected, abused or hurt child.

They feel helpless and ashamed on the inside but do not have a better way to channel their hurt than to inflict it on their siblings.

The Silent One has learned to be silent because, all their lives, their story could not be told. They were threatened by their siblings' violence, or no one would believe them.

Their only choice might have been to dissociate and bury the traumas deep within their bodies and souls. Later in life, their traumatic symptoms may show up as chronic fatigue, bodily pain, depression, or anxiety.

Rather than rightfully expressing their anger and setting boundaries, the Silenced One often blames themselves and internalizes the aggression they have suffered. They may become very harsh toward themselves and hear an inner critical voice that constantly puts them down. The Silence One may take the psychological scars and the internalized shame into adulthood and not feel legitimate as a person. They may not believe they deserve to be loved and sabotage opportunities and loving relationships. They may also become bullies to others, as a way of releasing the unprocessed resentment.

From my studies in psychology, I have named some of the dynamic relationships of siblings, which cause certain effects on us as an adult. In reading I saw myself and my siblings' dynamics, and relationships I saw the relationship dynamics in my own children, and my grandchildren. It really makes you look at why people act the way they do.

As we grow up as a child, we often sense that things are not right or fair, but we figure that it is all right, and you learn to live with it. Sometimes it just gradually creeps in, without warning and we do not realize what is happening to our families. We settle for certain behavior and accept things that we know are not right. Sadly, some people were not taught what is right and wrong. We accept unruly behavior or wrong doings, trying to keep everybody happy and at peace, and not rock the boat. Eventually we see where certain things should be talked about to correct the troubling attitudes and unruly behavior in our family members.

As parents we need to speak with love, even in discipline and never curse or call our children out of their names, like dumb, stupid or ugly. Negative words and actions cut at the heart and remain in the brain to haunt us. As time goes on some members may have problems of not feeling as loved as others, sometimes they may have low self-esteem, and feel they are not good enough or that they are good for nothing. Some may feel unattractive and compared to other members that are always told how beautiful they are. Sometimes they may have suffered traumatic experience like rape or made to feel dirty or unworthy because of these traumas. Sometimes they are ashamed and feel no one will listen to them or believe them, they could feel that they would just be blamed as if it were all their fault for being in the wrong place or dressing a certain way and they may feel like they are considered as a bad person . Sometimes they may be called ringleaders because everything that happens, they feel that they are blamed even if at times they were not involved. So, these are some of the situations that may arise in the family, and cause bouts of jealousy, envy and strife and misunderstanding in the family circle. We can also notice that some of the actual traumas , how they happen , when we look at the sibling dynamics , such as being a bully or being a silent one., The Golden Child and the Outcast, the mature one and the eternal child, are all mixed up in all of our lives.

We will study the word from the bible to see how our families from the bible handled some of the same issues. Did they do a great job , they knew God, but still allowed sin to creep in and cause havoc in their families, as we do often times, but they found that God is a God of mercy, and He can forgive us and put us back in right relations with each other and most importantly with Him . Let us study and see what happened in the beginning of time, how the drama was to play out on the stage that we call life.

 First of all, let us see what the Bible has to say about these dysfunctional families that may have these personality flaws. James 3:13-17" NIV 'Who is wise and understanding among you? Let them show it by their good life, by deeds done in the humility that comes from wisdom. But if you harbor bitter envy and selfish ambition in your hearts, do not boast about it or deny the truth. Such wisdom does not come down from heaven, but is earthly, unspiritual, and demonic.

For where you have envy and selfish ambition, there you find disorder and every evil practice. But the wisdom that comes from heaven is first of all; pure; then peace loving, considerate, submissive, full of mercy and good fruit, impartial and sincere. It is so easy to be drawn into the wrong desires by pressures of society, even by well-meaning Christians. By listening to advice to" assert yourself "," go for it"," set ambitious goals "we are drawn into greed and destructive competitiveness. Seeking God 's wisdom delivers us from the need to compare ourselves to others and to want what they have.

We want more possessions, more money, higher status, more recognition. When we do not get what we want, we try to undermine others in order to get what they have. We lie to try to discredit others, scandalize their name so we will look good. We are like crabs in a barrel, we are constantly climbing up and pushing or pulling others down to give us more leeway to the top. Instead of aggressively grabbing what we want, we should ask God to help us get rid of our selfish desires and trust him to give us what we really need. We may not need what others have because the price may be too high to pay, and we may not really want it that bad to walk in other 's shoes to obtain what they have. From my studying the Old Testament, I find all my best examples in the Bible. The Bible teaches us that we are all human and subject to sin. we want to do what is right in God's sight, but evil is always crouching at our door. There is a way that can get us there and that is the word and the teachings of God.

First, I would like to talk about where these tendencies of jealousy envy and strife actually took place, we will see how our heroes and heroines in the bible managed sin. They were like we are, sinful, but through God 's mercies and forgiveness taught us valuable lessons that we can learn and live our lives better and encourage and love and nurture and cherish our families, that none are lost.

It was actually in the beginning, that we see pride, jealousy, envy, and strife begin to rear its ugly head. When Satan was with GOD in heaven. Lucifer was a beautiful angel and was in charge of music. He became puffed up with pride. He wanted to be God, not to be a servant of God. Notice the I will statement Satan made in Isaiah 14: 12-15," How art thou fallen from heaven, O Lucifer, son of the morning!

How art thou cut down to the ground, which didst weaken the nations! For thou hast said in thine heart, I will ascend into heaven, I will exalt my throne above the stars of God: I will sit upon the mount of the congregation, in the sides of the North. I will ascend above the heights of the clouds, I will be like the Highest: Yet thou shalt be brought down to hell, to the sides of the pit."

Ezekiel 28:13 describes Lucifer as an exceedingly beautiful Angel.

Lucifer was the highest of all angels the anointed cherub the most beautiful of all of God's creatures, but he was not content in his position. Instead, Lucifer desired to be God and kick God off his throne and take over the rule of the universe. Lucifer wanted to be God and interesting enough that is essentially how Lucifer tempted Adam and Eve within the garden of Eden Genesis 31:5. How did Lucifer fall from heaven ?Actually a fall is not an accurate description, it would be far more accurate to say God cast Lucifer out of heaven Isaiah 14:15,NIV Ezekiel 28:16 - 17. "Through your widespread trade you were filled with violence, and you sinned. So, I drove you in disgrace from the mount of God and I expelled you, guardian cherub, from among the fiery stones. Your heart became proud on account of your beauty, and you corrupted your wisdom because of your splendor. I made a spectacle of you before kings. Satan did not fall from heaven Satan was pushed. Satan and the fallen angels were put out of heaven for good".

When God created the world, he made man, Adam, and breathe the breath of life into Adam. Adam became lonely and God had Adam to fall in a deep sleep and took a rib from Adam and formed his helpmate, Eve. Adam and Eve were so happy at first and had everything they needed. God had told them they could have any fruits from any of the trees but one. God forbade this tree. The tree of the knowledge of good and evil, we now see Adam and Eve in the garden of Eden, the garden that God had given them to live in forever.

Then one day Eve encounters Satan, disguised as a crafty serpent, Satan came to tempt Eve. Why does Satan tempt us? Temptation is Satan's invitation to give in to his kind of life and give up on God's kind of life. Satan tempted Eve and succeeded by making false promises to her by getting her to sin by eating the fruit from the forbidden tree.

We always want the one thing that is forbidden. Could Eve have resisted temptation? Yes, by following the same guidelines, we can follow them. First, we must realize that when you are tempted, it is not a sin. We have not sinned until we give in to temptation. Then, to resist temptation we must (1). Pray for strength to resist, (2) run, sometimes literally and (3) say no when confronted with what we know is wrong. James 1:12, tells of the blessings and rewards for those who do not give in when tempted. "Blessed Is the man that endured temptation: for when he is tried, he shall receive the crown of life, which the Lord hath promised to them that love Him." The serpent, Satan, tempted Eve by getting her to doubt God's goodness. He suggested that God was strict, stingy, and selfish for not wanting Eve to share his knowledge of good and evil. Satan made Eve forget all that God had given her and focus on the one thing she could not have. We fall into trouble, too when we focus on the few things, we do not have rather than on the countless things God has given us. The next time you are feeling sorry for yourself over what you do not have consider all you do have and be thankful to God for your many blessings.

 As soon as Eve had eaten the forbidden fruit, she found her husband Adam and begin to entice him to eat of the fruit because she knew deep down in her heart that she had done wrong and had sinned against God. One of the realities of sin is that its effects spread. After Eve sinned, she involved Adam in her wrongdoing. When we do something wrong, often we try to relieve our guilt by involving someone else. Like poison in a river, sin swiftly spreads.

Recognize and confess your sins to God before you are tempted to coerce others around you to sin., After Adam and Eve had eaten the forbidden fruit, they became ashamed and felt naked and found fig leaves to cover their nakedness. God started looking for them and called out Adam's name, Adam spoke and said that he was hiding because he was naked.

 God spoke to Adam and said, "who told you, that you were naked?' Adam knew that he had sinned, and disobeyed God and that God was not pleased with his disobedience. After sinning, Adam and Eve felt guilty and embarrassed over their nakedness. Their guilty feelings made them run from God and tried to hide. A guilty conscience is a warning signal God placed inside you that goes off when you've done wrong.

The worst thing you could do is drop the guilty feelings without dropping the cause. That is like using a pain killer but not addressing the disease. Be glad those guilty feelings are there; they make you aware of your sin, so you can ask God's forgiveness and then you can correct your wrongdoing by receiving God's forgiveness and mercy. Adam and Eve chose their course of action (disobedience) and then God chose His. As a holy God, he could respond only in a way consistent with His perfect moral nature. He could not allow sin to go unchecked, He had to punish them.

If the consequences of Adam and Eve's sin seem extreme, remember that their sin set in motion the world's constant tendency toward disobeying God. That is why we sin today: Every human being ever born, with the exception of Jesus, has inherited the sinful nature of Adam and Eve (Romans 5:12-21) Adam and Eve 's punishment reflects how seriously God views sin of any kind.

*Adam and Eve were put out of the garden of Eden .and they were giving the curse of the woman having to bear children and t*he men having to work by the sweat of their brow.

We now see how life was like for Adam and Eve being taken out of the Garden of Eden. Adam began to work the land and Eve had two sons. Cain was the oldest and he farmed the land as his father, Adam, did. Abel was the youngest child, and he was the first shepherd. Abel presented pleasing sacrifices to God. God was not as please with Cain's sacrifice. Conflicts between children in the family are going to happen. Siblings sometimes are competitive and try to outdo one another. Sometimes it causes conflict and fights among the siblings.

This is what happened with Cain and Abel. The Lord was pleased with Abel's sacrifice of his firstling of sheep, but He was not pleased with Cain's sacrifice of the fruit of the earth. God gave Cain a chance to make a better sacrifice but instead he became angry and furious with Abel. In other words, Cain became jealous and envious of Abel; he wanted praise. Cain's reaction gives us a clue that his attitude was wrong from the start.

 Remember sin had already entered in the world by Adam and Eve, therefore their children were not excluded from sin. Cain had a choice to make. He could try to make his sacrifice more pleasing to God. A correct decision is a clear reminder of how often we are aware of opposite choices.

Yet we sometimes make the wrong choice out of anger just as Cain did. The family was destroyed at that time, Abel was dead, and God marked Cain, and Cain asked to be sent away, so that he would not be harmed by others because of the mark he had for murdering his brother. This was the first sin of murder committed by Cain. Although the Lord bless Adam and Eve with more children this was a breakdown in the family unit., we may not be choosing to murder like Cain , but if we allow jealousy to fester in our hearts it can lead to murder of someone's character or someone's livelihood.

We should be in control of our anger and not let it get out of hand. This is a great example of jealousy, envy and strife, these feelings motivating our behavior cannot always be changed by simple thought-power. But here we begin to experience God's willingness to help. Asking God for His help to do what is right and to take the jealousy and bitterness out of our hearts which can prevent us from doing what we will regret later. **

Another example of families that got out of hand by not trusting God and literally not listening and believing God's words. In the bible we learn Abraham was considered a faithful and obedient servant of God. Because of his faith in God, God gave Abraham a promise of having multitudes descendants in the promise land. Now this story takes place as Abraham moves out of his country of Ur because God told him to move, he was obedient and moved out and he took his wife Sarah and his nephew Lot to journey to another country to fulfill God's promise to Abraham.

In the process of moving, we see that Abraham became a little intimidated and afraid when they came through Egypt and the Pharoah looked on his wife Sarah with favor and saw that she was beautiful   and wanted her. Abraham was afraid to tell Pharoah that she was his wife because he felt he would be killed, so he said it was his sister, and she was taken to his house.

The king realized he was being tormented by terrible things happening when he found out that Sarah was Abraham's wife. The king knew if he had touched Sarah, he would have more strange things happen to him.

Why did Abraham lie about Sarah being his wife, one reason was because he was afraid, Abraham knew the king would kill him, and he knew his wife was coveted by this king. He also felt like he was just telling a harmless lie because she was also his half-sister. This brought about strife because the king did not know that this   was   Abraham's wife. He wanted someone he was not supposed to have and Abraham instead of telling the truth could have caused the king great danger. So, the king was terribly angry with Abraham, but he gladly let Abraham and Sarah go because he did not want any more trouble. The king gladly gave them great gifts to take on their journey and leave his country.

Sometimes we have to be willing to speak up and tell the truth in spite of the circumstances and truly trust God to be our defender and help us in our situation , so that we can avoid lies and fear that can sometimes put us in grave danger and effect our relationship with God.

Now we find out that as years go by there were a lot of drama and situations that happened during Abraham's life. One of the things that comes out is that God had promised Abraham an heir that would inherit this land God had promised. Abraham's descendants would multiply as the sand of the land. Abraham and Sarah, we're getting very old and thought I it was impossible to have a child at their age, but we know that all things are possible with God and nothing is too hard for God. , Sarah being like most of us wanted to help God because, she knew at her age she was barren and saw no other way humanly possible for this to happen, so because of how impatient she was, a suggestion was made to Abraham to have her maid servant , Hagar and to have a baby ad this would be the baby that God had promised.

Hagar became pregnant but all the strife, the jealousy, and the envy that came about could been avoided if they had waited on God. So, we see now these three ugly heads of jealousy, envy and strife rearing to complicate our lives because we do not trust totally in God. So now what happens, Hager is pregnant, she is showing disrespect to Sarah, and Sarah is not pleased. Sarah is jealous, she's envious of the baby that Hagar is giving to Abraham and her, she is really not feeling any part of it.

Sarah becomes very angry, disrespected, and ruthless in her dealing with Hagar, and she voices her dislike to Abraham concerning how Hagar is treating her. She begins to blame Abraham for this mishap.

Remember bringing others in and blaming others help us to feel less guilty of our wrongdoings. Abraham reminds her that this was her idea, and he simply went along with it. Of course, Abraham could have spoken up and refuse to be involved with Hagar and continued to wait on God. Abraham sent Hagar away to have her baby, feeling alone and downtrodden and God met her at the place she had wandered to. God found and call her by name and told her to go back to Abraham and Sarah and have her baby and that her son would be head of a nation also.

Hagar was obedient and went back and had her son Ishmael man, who would become a very wild and untamed as a wild donkey! Genesis 16;16 Before Ishmael was born, the angel of the Lord told Hagar, "This son of yours will be as a wild man, as untamed as a wild donkey. He will raise his fist against everyone, and everyone will be against him. Yes , he will live in open hostility against all his relatives' So as time went on Sarah did become pregnant as God had promised and she had a son name Isaac, which means laughter and they were so happy with the promise son God had given them in His own time. Ishmael was very unkind to Isaac and would often tease him, possibly because of his jealousy of Isaac. Sarah told Abraham to put them out and he sent them away with meager means and they left, and they ended up in Egypt, so this story definitely tells us about jealousy envy and strife and how this family let it grow into what is now and international threat to the world. Two nations, in the Middle East divided over what happened in the biblical days. There again we must trust totally in God and believe what the word says. It might not be in our timing, but God is always on time without our help. We must have patience to wait on God and believe in His promises to make the difference in our lives and avoid the pitfalls of jealousy, envy, and strife. **

Our next example given in the Bible is when Abraham found a wife for Isaac. Abraham sent his servant Eliezer to his homeland to find a wife for Isaac, to avoid him intermarrying with a heathen neighbor.

He gave the servant special instructions and so the servant went to the land of Abraham's family and followed Abraham's instructions for Isaac wife.

His servant found Rebecca and she matched all his qualifications, and he knew she was the one... Rebecca left with Eliezer to become Isaac's wife. Years went by and Rebecca seemed as though she could not have children at first, but Isaac prayed to the Lord, and she became pregnant. While during her pregnancy she noticed the babies jostled each other within her womb and she asked the Lord, why is this. Gen.25:23" The Lord said to her, two nations are in your womb, and two peoples from within you will be separated; one people will be stronger than the other, and the older will serve the younger.'

When the twins were born, Esau came out first, he was very hairy and red, and Jacob came out next holding on to Esau's heel, seeming to want to pull Esau back.

Sometimes we see these things with our kids when they are young, one is more aggressive than the other. Some may be timid, some intellectual and some a little sassy. We should give special attention to each child that they may have what they need to grow and mature in the nurturing and admonition of the Lord. Most important, that they may know and do the purpose of God's will for their life. I believe when you have your children many of their traits and actions that are displayed are part of their makeup and the DNA from the mother and the father which means some good and some bad genes. Your children have the propensity to inherit some of the things you inherited, like a propensity to some bad habits, such as lying, alcoholism, drugs, and mental health. They are also prone to having some of the same health issues we have. Therefore, we should take stock into who we are and what we bring to the table and yes this means anything that is not pleasing to God we need to begin to pray about these things and let God show us how we need to love , nurture and discipline and build up our children. We should not take pride in the fact that they are just like us if we know we are not doing God's will.

Esau and Jacob, who were two vastly different people they look quite different although they were twins Esau was reddish and very hairy what we might call him a manly man and he was a skillful hunter. Jacob was fairer and hairless, unlike his brother. He was a momma's boy and stayed around close to his mother, but he was very slick and sly. Because Isaac loved the taste of wild game, and the fact that Esau was a hunter he favored Esau and Rebecca favored Jacob.

Rebecca remembered what God had told her when she was caring them that Jacob would be greater than his brother caused her to show favoritism among her boys. Jacob always had an idea to get ahead and to hustle his way through to get what he wanted. Now Esau was a simple type of man of nature man that was fairly more honest and careless. He was not a schemer, or dreamer. Jacob was even able to hustle and bargain to get Esau's birthright. Esau was hungry and Jacob had made some porridge and because of Esau being hungry at that moment, he agreed to sell his birthright for a plate of porridge to satisfy his basic need of hunger, not thinking or caring at the moment, what he was being proposition. He lived in the moment.

Esau was relaxed and was not a planner. So, now we see the personality of each son. Do you think these relationships panned out? Now we have to know a little bit about his mother Rebecca and her family. Rebecca was from a family that you might say were slickers' plotters and schemers. We will learn later of the trickery that came out and tore up the family and brought about jealousy, envy, and strife.

As the story goes on. let us examine Rebecca and Issacs' family. First of all, there was a little favoritism going on. Rebecca favored Jacob. Jacob was a momma's boy. Isaac favored Esau because he loved the fact that Esau was a burly hunter, and he would capture game for the stew he loved.

Conflict was already rearing its ugly head. I know there is favoritism among our children and family. We as parents need to be more aware of this and try too not to be so obvious about it. We must also realize that each child is different, some more loving, some more mischievous, and not as loving. So, we must try to figure out why that is.

Like I said earlier in the text we sometimes simplify some of the behavior of a child and we may think it is cute and encourage it, or do they remind you of some of the things about your childhood , that you don't like and don't like to see them patterning after some of our mistakes and some of the bad habits we may have shown up in our childhood. The child may remind you of another relative, that had some of the same attributes; they ended up using them for good or for bad. We may be a little sterner and harsher with them, to try and keep their misguided behaviors from growing into something that might hold them back in life or cause destruction for them. This may make the kids feel like you do not love them as much, but it must be done in love and always let them know you love them, and you know they can do better. It is our parental duty to try to raise our kids to be kind and have integrity and think of others as well as yourself. We must be careful how we talk to our kids. They should not hear us talk about people of the family or anyone and show mercy to others and teach your children that God is the source of all they will ever need.

 We should always be loving in our correction and discipline and never put them.

down or caused them to feel less than anyone else and always tell them and show them how much you love them and teach them about the love of God, mercy and grace that He shows us every day.

Back to the story of Isaac and Rebecca. We see another pattern of family similarities; Isaac also meets a king in his travels to avoid a famine. This was the same thing that happened to his father Abraham. The king saw his wife, Rebecca, and because she was also beautiful, the king wanted her, and Isaac lied and said it was his sister and so the king would not kill him. The king found out when he saw Isaac was affectionate to Rebecca, Isaac was summoned, and had to answer the king for the lie, he told. We find dishonesty, disrespect, lying deception, trickery, and all-around dysfunctional mayhem. Isaac and Rebecca loved each other, but their children got in the way of trust and loyalty.

Rebecca was aware that God's plan would be channeled through Jacob, not Esau (Genesis 25:23), And the Lord said unto her ". It is like you are rooting against each other, with your sons, and this does not seem like a part of a happy and loving union. Sometimes the fruit does not fall far from the tree. I believe in knowing the story about Rebecca's brother, Laban, which will be discussed later, he was a known swindler and liar. It seems like DNA might have played a part in the little scheme that Jacob and his mother had cooked up to fool Esau out of his blessing. Isaac had weaknesses too. Under pressure he tended to lie, in conflict he looked to avoid confrontation, and he also played favorites between his sons and alienated his wife. Although we know Isaac was the patriarch, Rebecca had the power in their relationship. Rather than stand his ground, Isaac found it easier to compromise or lie to avoid confrontations. Esau was so careless and unconcern he sold his birthright to Jacob for some porridge because he was hungry at that particular time, no regard for what that would mean to him in the future.

 Jacob was always trying to get a hustle and have gains for himself. Oh, what a tangled web we weave, when we practice deceiving. These unpleasant habits have a way of catching up with you. Now, Isaac is getting old, and his eyesight is failing him. He calls Esau his favorite and tells him to go hunting to get venison, so that he can make him a delicious stew of venison. He realized he was getting old, and he wanted to bless Esau, since he was the oldest. Mine you, there were listening to this conversation. As Esau obediently leaves to get his father's wishes granted a plot begins to develop. The plot was none other than Rebecca and Jacob cooking up a plan to take Esau's inheritance and blessing from him. Jacob tried to dissuade his mother from carrying this deceitful plan out, but she was sure it would work because of Issacs's blindness. Jacob reminded his mother that he and Esau were made up differently and Esau was very hairy, and his father could tell them apart by touching them.

Rebecca preceded to tell Jacob to get a goat and clean him and she took the skins to cover Jacob, so he could feel hairy, and she cooked up the stew for Jacob to take to his father and get the blessing.

How shrewd a woman, she must have been? How many family members will go to extra trouble to make something happen for their child.? This is favoritism with a big bang. You have now caused your son to lie, you have been dishonest and disloyal to your husband. How do you explain such an atrocity to the other child?

How does it make the other child feel, to know you would try to move, heaven and earth to give them what is not rightfully theirs? The Bible makes us think and shows us the frailty and selfishness of our human natures. God must guide us to manage all situations and listen and do what he tells you, rather than doing things our way.

Rebecca made the stew quickly and Jacob took the stew to Isaac to eat. Although Isaac was a little puzzled. Even though Isaac could not see well, he did notice the smell of Jacob, so he wanted to feel him and once he felt like Esau, although Jacob

did not sound like him and he was surprised that Esau had gotten to him earlier than expected.

Isaac was satisfied with the stew and gave Jacob , Esau 's blessing, after Jacob left feeling that the plan had worked, Esau came to his father Isaac with the stew and his father realize that he had been fooled and he had given the blessing that should have been to Esau' to his second born Jacob. Esau was devastated, so angry at Jacob and his parents.

He wanted to kill Jacob, and he angered his parents by marrying Canaanite women because he knew his father did not want Jacob to marry them, so he chose to get even by marrying more Canaanite women. Meanwhile Rebecca realizes that Esau was enraged with Jacob and wanted to kill him, so she hastily prepared to send Jacob away to her brother, Laban so he would stay.

away until Esau had time to cool off. How we react to a moral dilemma often exposes our real motives. Frequently we are more worried about being caught than about doing what is right. Jacob did not seem concerned about the deceitfulness of his mother's plan; instead, he was afraid of getting in trouble while carrying it out. If you are worried about getting caught, you are in a position that is less than honest. Let your fear of getting caught be a warning to do right. Jacob paid a high price for caring out his dishonest plan.

 Sin had trapped Rebecca and was degrading her character. Correcting yourself in the middle of doing wrong can bring hurt and disappointments, but it also brings freedom from sin though Jacob got the blessing he wanted, deceiving his father cost him dearly. These are the consequences of that deceit.   #1, He never saw his mother that he loved so much   again, #2. His brother wanted to kill him, #3He was deceived by his uncle, Laban #4his family became torn with strife, #5 Esau became the founder of an enemy nation #6 Jacob was exiled from his family for years.

 Ironically, Jacob would have received the birthright and blessing anyway. Imagine how different his life, could have been if his mother had allowed God to do things his way, and in his time. He would have been able to enjoy his mother's life, not knowing when he left, he would never see her again. He and his brother could have really enjoyed brotherly love, his family was torn apart, and Esau founded a nation that were enemies with him.

 There are times when we try to justify the things we choose to do. Often, we try to add God's approval to our actions. We are responsible for what we do and must always be cautious about our motives. When thinking about a course of action, are you simply seeking God's stamp of approval on something you have already decided to do? Initiative and action are admirable and right when they are control by God's wisdom. Our actions must be guided by God's word. God even makes use of our mistakes in His plan. Parental favoritism hurts a family. Remember jealousy, envy and strife take its toll on a family, even down through generations.

As Jacob was on his way to his uncle Laban home, he had a dream. Genesis 28:13-15 " And the Lord spoke to Jacob, and said I am the Lord God of Abraham and the God of Isaac , the land where thou liest , to thee will I give it, and to thy seed shall be as dust of the earth, and thou shall spread abroad to the west , and to the east and to the North and the South: and in thee and in thy seed shall all the families of the earth be blessed.

And behold I am with thee and will keep thee in all places whither thou goest and will bring thee again into this land; for I will not leave thee until I have done that which I have spoken to thee of." Genesis 28: 20- "And Jacob vowed a vow saying, If God will be with me and will keep me in this way that I go and will give the bread to eat and raiment to

 put on. So that I come again to my father's house in peace; then shall the Lord be my God; and of all that thou shalt give me I will surely give the tenth unto thee." According to one commentary, it was suggested that Jacob may have tried to bargain with God. It is possible that he, in his ignorance of how to worship and serve God, treated God like a servant who would perform a service for a tip.

More, likely Jacob was not bargaining but pledging his future to God. He may have been saying, in effect "Since you blessed, I will follow you" Whether Jacob was bargaining or pledging, God blessed him. But God also had some difficult lesson for Jacob to learn. As Stated before, Rebecca 's brother, Laban was a trickster just like Rebecca and Jacob, and Jacob would soon find out the hard way.

 When Laban met Jacob, and he told him the story of what had happen and why his mother had sent him to live with him Laban made a statement Genesis 29:14" And Laban said to him, surely, thou art my bone and my flesh', realizing that Jacob had some of his same DNA of trickery. Laban had two daughters, Rachel, and Leah. Rachel was beautiful and fair, and Leah was the oldest and not considered as attractive as Rachel. When Jacob arrived there and met Rachel, he at once fell in love with her, even though she was his first cousin, but that was the custom in Biblical times.

Jacob asked Laban about marrying Rachel and Laban told Jacob he could work seven years for her, and he was happy to do this. Jacob thought he was on the up and up, but we must remember, when we do wrong it can come back to haunt us. Fast forward, seven years were up, and Jacob prepares to marry Rachel.

The ceremony was over, and Jacob went into the marriage bed for his wife Rachel, after they had consummated the wedding, and Jacob realized that he had not married Rachel but Leah instead. Jacob was so angry when he went to Laban and wanted to know what had happened and why he had tricked him when he had held up his part of the bargain. Laban tried to explain that he had forgotten to mention the custom that since Leah was the oldest and not married yet, he had to give her a way to be married first before Rachel. This explanation really did not satisfy Jacob, because he really loved Rachel and wanted her for his wife. So, there was another deal made by Laban, which would guarantee his marriage to Rachel if he worked another seven years. This meant that it would be another seven years for Jacob to work for Laban in order to ensure this union. Jacob really loved Rachael more than Leah.

The Lord saw how lonely and how bad Leah felt about Jacob's love for Rachel, that God opened Leah's womb, and she had a son and named him Reuben. Leah continued to have Simeon, Levi, and Judah.

She felt that having these sons for Jacob would make him love her more than Rachel, but he still loved Rachel more, here we see how Leah was made to feel unwanted and low self-esteem due to not feeling loved by her husband, but with Laban tricking Jacob, and fooling him by switching his daughters at the marriage.

How the deception in families again causes jealousy, envy, and strife. Rachel found out that she was barren and without child, and it made her desperately compete with her sister Leah for Jacob 's affection, thinking because Leah had given him children that made Leah more important to Jacob. She was trying to gain from Jacob what he had already given her: his devoted love. Here we see two sisters at each other's house, one feeling unloved and the other feeling disappointed because she cannot give her husband children.

Then we have Jacob in between two sisters trying to make them both happy. Then we have Laban, the father of the two girls, who have gotten double dowries from two marriages that he had not be truthful about has cause division, jealousy, envy, and strife, and don't forget the greed from Laban.

Rachel and Leah were in a cruel contest. In their race to have more children, they both gave their servant girls to Jacob as concubines. Remember, Jacob's grandmother, the same thing happens with Sarah and Abraham, Sarah gave her maid servant to Abraham to give them a child. Jacob would have been wise to refuse, even though this was an accepted custom of the day. The fact that a custom is socially acceptable does not mean it is wise or right. You will be spared much heartbreak if you look at the potential consequences, to you or others, for your actions. Are you doing anything that might cause future problems? Eventually the Lord answered Rachel's prayers and gave her a child of her own. In the meantime, however, she had taken matters into her own hands by giving her servant girl to Jacob. Trusting God when nothing seems to happen is difficult. But it is harder still to live with the consequences of taking matters into our own hands. Resist the temptation to think God has forgotten you. Have patience and courage to wait for God.

Jacob worked extremely hard for Laban and made Laban and himself very wealthy. Jacob's wealth made Laban's son very jealous. It is sometimes difficult to be happy when others are doing better than we are. Comparing our success with that of others is a dangerous way to judge the quality of our lives. By comparing ourselves to others, we may be giving jealousy a foothold.

We can avoid jealousy by rejoicing in others' success. (see Rom 12:15). Although Laban treated Jacob unfairly, God still increased Jacob prosperity. God's power is not limited by lack of fair play.

He has the ability to meet our needs and make us thrive even though others mistreat us, to give in and respond unfairly in return is to be no different from your enemies.

Leaving home was not difficult for Rachel and Leah because their father had treated them as poorly as he had Jacob. According to custom, they were supposed to receive the benefits of the dowry Jacob paid for them, which was 14 years of arduous work. When Laban did not give them what was rightfully theirs, they knew they would never inherit anything from their fathers. Thus, they wholeheartedly approved of Jacob's plan to take the wealth he had gained and leave.

The last time Jacob had seen Esau, his brother was ready to kill hm for stealing the family blessing (Gen25:29-27:42). Esau was so angry he had vowed to kill Jacob as soon as their father Isaac was dead (Gen 27:41). Fearing their reunion, Jacob sent a messenger ahead with gifts. He hoped to buy Esau's favor. How would you feel if you had cheated someone out of their inheritance, his most precious possession? and you knew you were about to meet this person. Jacob had taken Esau's birthright (Gen,25:33 and his blessing (Gen 27:27-40). Now 20 years later he was about to meet his brother for the first time, and he was full of anxiety and fear. He collected his thoughts and decided to pray. When we face a difficult conflict, we can run around frantically, or we can pause to pray. Which approach do you think will be more effective?

 Genesis 32: 22-29, "Jacob arose that night and took his two wives and his two women servants, and his eleven sons, and passed over the ford Jabbok. And he took them and sent them over the brook and sent over all that he had. And Jacob was left alone; and there wrestled a man with him until the breaking of the day. And when he saw that he prevailed not against him, he touched the hollow of his thigh, and the hollow of Jacob's thigh was out of joint, as he wrestled with him. And he said I will not let thee go; except thou bless me. And he said unto him, what is thy name? And he said Jacob.

And he said thy name shall be called no more Jacob, but Israel: for as a prince hast, thou power with God and with men and hast prevailed. And Jacob asked, he said Tell me I pray thee, thy name.

 And he said Wherefor is it that thou dost asked after my name. And he blessed him there." Jacob continued his wrestling match all night just to be blessed. He was persistent. God encourages persistence in all areas of our lives. Including the spiritual life do you need more persistence? Strong character results from struggling under tough conditions.

God gave many Biblical people new names (Abraham, Sarah, Peter). Their new names were a symbol of how God had changed their lives.

Here we see Jacob's character had changed. Jacob, the ambitious deceiver had now become Israel, the prince who struggles with God and prevails.

It is refreshing to see Esau's change of heart when the two brothers meet again. The bitterness over losing his birthright and blessing (Genesis 27: 36-41) seems to have gone. Instead, Esau is content with what he has. Jacob even exclaims how great it is to see his brother obviously pleased with him (Genesis 33:10) Life can deal us some bad situations. We can feel cheated, as Esau did, but we do not have to remain bitter. We can remove bitterness from our lives by honestly expressing our feelings to God, forgiving those who have wronged us, and being content with what we have. Esau greeted his brother Jacob, with a great hug. Imagine how hard this must have been for a man who once had actually plotted his brother's death. (Genesis 27:41). But time away from each other allowed the bitter wounds to heal. With the passing of time, each brother was able to see that their relationship was more important than their real estate.

Abraham, Isaac, and Jacob are among the most significant people in the Old Testament. It is important to realize that this significance is not based upon their personal characters, but upon the character of God. They were all men who earned the grudging respect and even fear of their peers; they were wealthy, and powerful, and yet each was capable of lying, deceit and selfishness. They were not the perfect heroes we might have expected; instead, they were just like us, trying to please God but often falling short. Jacob was the third in line of God's plan to start a nation from Abraham. The success of that plan was more often in spite of, rather than because of Jacob's life.

Before Jacob was born, God promised that his plan would be worked out through Jacob, and not his twin brother, Esau.

Although Jacob's methods were not always respectable, his skill, determination, and patience have to be admired. As we follow him from birth to death, we are able to see God's work. Jacob's life had four stages, each marked by a personal encounter with God. In the first stage, Jacob lived up to his name, which means 'one who supplants, undermines or grabs '. He grabbed Esau's heel at birth, and by the time he fled from home, he had also grabbed his brother's birthright and blessing. During his flight, God first appeared to him. Not only did God confirm to Jacob his blessing, but he awakened in Jacob's a personal knowledge of himself.

In the second stage, Jacob experienced life from the other side, being manipulated and deceived by Laban. But there is a curious change: The Jacob of stage one would have simply left Laban, whereas the Jacob of the stage two, after deciding to leave waited six years for God's permission., In the third stage , Jacob was in a new role as grabber, this time by the Jordan River , he grabbed on to God and wouldn't let go . He realized his dependence on the God who had continued to bless him. His relationship to God became essential to his life, and his name change to Israel, "A prince who prevails with God." Jacob's last stage of life was to be grabbed God achieved a firm hold on him. In responding to Joseph's invitation to come to Egypt, Jacob was clearly unwilling to make a move without God's approval.

After a joyful reunion with his brother, Esau (who journeyed from Edom) Jacob set up camp in Succoth. Later he moved on to Shechem where his daughter, Dinah, the daughter of Leah was raped and two of his sons took revenge on the city. The two that took revenge on Shechem were Simeon and Levi. Dinah, the daughter of Leah, went out to see the women of the land. And when this man named Shechem, the son of Hamor, who was the Hivite prince of the country saw her, and he took her and raped her. Shechem may have been a victim of love at first sight, but his actions were impulsive and evil. Not only did he sin against Dinah, but he also sinned against the entire family.

The consequences of his deed were severe both for him and for Jacob. Even Shechem declared love for Dinah could not excuse the evil he did by raping her. Do not allow sexual passion to boil over into evil actions. Passion must be controlled. Simeon was able to slaughter about all the men in the town singlehanded with the help of Levi. They came up with a solution , to get back at

Shechem , since he wanted to marry Dinah and his father also agreed to this union, that all the men would have to be circumcised before he could marry Dinah, and while all the men and and Shechem were recovering from the circumcision, and unarmed, Levi and Simeon went in and attacked all the men and killed them .

They took all the spoils and all the women from the town and Jacob was so angry when he found out what they had done.

In seeking revenge against Shechem, Simeon and Levi lied, stole, and murdered. Their desire for justice was right but their ways of achieving it were wrong. Because of their sin, their father cursed them with his dying breath. A generation later, their descendants lost part of the Promised land that was allotted to them. When tempted to return evil for evil, leave revenge to God and spare yourself the dreadful consequences of sin.

Why did Simeon and Levi take such harsh action against the city of Shechem? Jacob's family saw themselves as set apart from others. God wanted them to remain separate from their heathen neighbors. But the brothers wrongly thought that being set apart meant being better. This arrogant attitude led to the terrible slaughter of innocent people. Dinah's brothers were outraged and took revenge on them. Pain, deceit, and murder followed. Sexual sin is no more than any other sin, but its consequences may be especially devastating.

Genesis 35: 16-19 "And while they journeyed to Bethel, and there was but a little way to come to Ephrath: and Rachel travailed, and she had hard labor. And it came to pass, when she was in hard labor, that the midwife said unto her, Fear not; thou shall have this son also. And it happened as her soul was un departing (for she died) that she calls his name Ben-oni: but his father calls him Benjamin. Rachel died and was buried in Ephrath, which is called Bethlehem."

Genesis 35: 21-22, "And Israel journeyed and spread his tent beyond the tower of Edar. And it came to pass, when Israel dwelt in that land, that Rueben, went and lay with Bilhah his father 's concubine and Israel heard it."

Many people believe that Christianity should offer a problem free life. Consequently, as life gets tough, they draw back disappointed.

Instead, they should decide to prevail with God through life 's storms. Problems and difficulties are painful but inevitable; you might as well see them as opportunities for growth. You cannot prevail with God unless you have troubles to prevail over.

Reuben's sin was costly, although not immediate. As the oldest son, he stood to receive a double part of the family inheritance and a place of leadership among his people. Reuben may have thought he got away with his sin. No more in mentioned of it until Jacob, on his deathbed, assembled his family for the final blessing.

Suddenly Jacob took away Reuben's double part and gave it to someone else. The reason? "Thou wentest up to thy father's bed, then defilest thou it " Gen49:4. Sin's consequences can plague us long after the sin is committed. When we do something wrong, we may think we can escape unnoticed, only to discover later that sin has been quietly breeding dire consequences.

Now the sons of Jacob were twelve, the sons of Leah; Reuben, Jacob's firstborn, and Simeon, Levi, and Judah, and Issachar, Zebulun and also a daughter Dinah, the sons of Rachel were Joseph and
Benjamin, and the sons of Bilhah, Rachel' handmaid was Dan, Naphtali, and the sons of Zilpha. Leah's handmaid; Gad and Asher.

The Edomites were descendants of Esau, who lived south and east of the Dead Sea. The country featured rugged mountains and desolate wilderness. Several major roads led through Edom, for it was rich in natural resources. During the Exodus, God told Israel to leave the Edomites alone (, Deut2:4, 5) because they were brethren. But Edom refused to let them enter the land, and later became bitter enemies of King David. We see how things that happen in the past rise up to cause us problems in the future. The nation of Edom and Israel shared the same ancestors, Isaac, and the same border. Israel looked down on the Edomites because they intermarried with the Canaanites.

God reminded Jacob of his new name, Israel which meant "a prince who prevails with God.'

.

There were many situations and things that happened with Jacob, now known as Israel, had to deal with his children as many of us do.

We all are so familiar with the story of Joseph, who was the first child of Rachel, and he was incredibly special to Israel. As a youngster, Joseph was overconfident. His natural self-assurance, increased by being Jacob's favorite son and by knowing of God's design on his life, was unbearable to his ten older brothers, who eventually conspired against him. We all know about Joseph's colorful coat Jacob had made for him. The coat became a symbolism of Jacob's favoritism toward Joseph, and it aggravated the already strained relationship between joseph and his brothers. Favoritism in families may be unavoidable, but its divisive effects should be minimized. Parents may not be able to change their feelings toward a favorite child, but they can change their actions toward the others. Joseph's brothers were already angry over the possibility of being ruled by their little brother because of his dreams of having them bow down to him, that he vividly expresses to them. Joseph fueled the fire with his immature attitude and boastful manner. No one enjoys braggart.

Joseph learned his lesson the hard way. His angry brothers sold him into slavery to get rid of him. After several years of hardship, Joseph learned an important lesson; Since our talent and knowledge come from God, it is more proper to thank him for them than to brag about them.

Could jealousy ever make you want to kill someone? Before saying, of course not, look at what happened in this story. Ten men were willing to kill their brother over a coat and because of his dreams. Their deep jealousy had grown into ugly rage, blinding them completely to what was right, Jealousy can be hard to recognize, because our reasons for it seem to make sense.

 But left unchecked, jealousy grows quickly and leads to serious sins. The longer you cultivate jealous feelings, the harder it is to uproot them. The time to deal with jealousy is when you notice yourself keeping score of what others have.

To cover their evil action, Jacob's sons deceived their father into thinking Joseph was dead. Jacob himself had deceived others many times (including his own father). Now though blessed by God, he still had to face the consequences of his sins. God may not have punished Jacob at once for his sins of deceit, but the consequences came nevertheless and stayed with him for the rest of his life.

Fast forward, Joseph had been sold at the age of 17 years old, now at 30 years Joseph rose to governor of Egypt. It was not easy getting there, but Joseph rose quickly to the top, from the prison walls to Pharaoh's palace. Pharaoh recognized that Joseph was a man" in whom the spirit of God is." You will not get to t interpret dreams for a king, but those who know you should be able to see God in you, through your kind words, merciful acts, and wise advice. Do your relatives, neighbors, and co-workers see you as a person in whom the spirit of God is? Joseph' training for this eminent position involved being first a slave, and then a prisoner. In each situation he learned the importance of serving God and others. Whatever your situation, no matter how undesirable consider it part of your training program for serving God.

Although Joseph's brothers had wanted to get rid of him. God used even their evil actions to fulfill his ultimate plan. He sent Joseph ahead to preserve their lives. After all, due to Joseph's interpretation of pharaohs dreams he interpreted that there would be famines in the lands and due to this revelation from God he was able to prepare Egypt for the famine , which his brothers and their family were able to buy food to sustain their families not even knowing Joseph was in charge of all the food they were able to buy. Joseph saves Egypt and prepare the way for the beginning of the nation of Israel. God is sovereign. His plans are not dictated by human actions.

 When others intend evil toward you, remember that they are only God's tools. As Joseph said to his brothers, "Ye thought evil against me; but God meant it unto good."

Joseph was rejected, kidnapped, enslaved, and imprisoned. Although his brothers had been unfaithful to him, he graciously forgave them and shared his prosperity with them. Joseph proved how God forgives us and showers us with goodness, even though we have sinned against Him. The same forgiveness and blessings are ours if we ask for them.

The faithfulness of Joseph affected his entire family. When he was in the pit and in prison, Joseph mut have wondered about his future., instead of despairing, he faithfully obeyed God and did what was right. Here we see one of the exciting results. We may not always see the effects of our faith, but we can be sure that God will honor faithfulness.

After hearing the joyful news that Joseph was alive, Jacob packed up and moved his family to Egypt. Stopping first in Beer-Sheba Jacob offered sacrifices and received assurance from God that Egypt was where he should go, Jacob and his family, settled in the land of Goshen, in the northeastern part of Egypt.

Jacob died; He lived to be 147 years old. Jacob spoke of God as one who fed him throughout his life. In his old age, he could clearly see his dependence upon God, this marks a total attitude change from that of his scheming and dishonest youth. To develop an attitude like Jacob's be willing to be fed. When you realize that every good thing comes from God, you lose any reason to try to grab it for yourself. Remember.

Jealousy, envy, and strife do not belong in our families. God will work things out His way and we may not have to suffer as much and see our families suffer or be destroyed. Take heed and let God be our guide. But also   Remember the sins of the parent are often repeated and amplified in their children.

We have studied and talked about God's word and saw how family relationships are affected by our impatience, our jealousy, our strife, and wrath on family to obtain what we want and have things our way. We do not consider what God wants and that He is quite able to bless   to deliver His promises, but we must learn to trust Him and wait on His timing. We have seen in prior reading how family dynamics may cause deceit, envy, jealousy, strife, wrath and even murder in families. We will now take a look at different relationships in the realm of authority, governing, and friends. We will still see how these things affect our family relations. We will talk about the evils that beset mankind, even when God guides us. We choose to do our own things and see what devastation comes from it. During this time there was a judge, name Samuel, he had ruled Israel well and saved them from the Philistines and led them back to God. By this time Samuel was an old man and appointed his sons to judge over Israel in his place, but they turned out to be corrupt. It does not state why Samuels's sons were bad, but we do know Eli was held responsible for his son's corruption. Eli was a high priest that mentored Samuel from a child unto adulthood. It is impossible to know if Samuel was a bad parent. His children were old enough to be on their own. We need to be careful not to blame ourselves for the sins of our children. On the other hand, parenthood is a formidable responsibility, and nothing should take greater priority than molding and shaping the lives of our children. The nation declared unto Samuel that they did not want another judge. Instead, they demanded to be given a king in order to be like other nations around them.

Saul was chosen to be king by the casting of lots, which was called the Urim and Thumim. Since the Israelites demanded a king God allowed Samuel to cast lots and Saul was then anointed as king. God knew this would not turn out great, but sometimes He gives us what we ask for, even when he knows we do not need it. Israel's true king was God, but the nation demanded another. Imagine wanting a human being instead of God. Often times we find ourselves wanting a man to lead us instead of God, because we want wealth , position , lustful pleasures, and do not want to obey God's laws.   , We know the words says we must obey God rather than man, and obedience is better than sacrifice.

First impressions can be very deceiving, especially when the images created by a person's appearance are contradicted by his or her qualities and abilities. Saul presented the ideal visual image of a king, but the tendencies of his character often went contrary to God's commands for a king. Saul was God's chosen leader, but this did not mean he was capable of being a king on his own. This makes me think of how sometimes we feel like we can do things in our own power and wisdom. We find that without God we cannot do anything. We must seek God's wisdom and His spirit to complete the work he has for us to do. This is the only way we will succeed and please God, not by might, but my spirit says the Lord. During his reign, Saul had his greatest successes when he obeyed God. His greatest failures resulted from acting on his own. Saul had the raw materials to be a good leader- appearance, courage, and action. Even his weaknesses could have been used by God if Saul had recognized them and left them in God's hands. His own choices cut him off from God and eventually alienated him from his own people.

From Saul we learn that while our strengths and abilities make us useful, it is our weaknesses that make us usable. Our skills and talents make us tools, but our failures and shortcomings remind us that we need a Craftsman in control of our lives. Whatever we accomplish on our own is only a hint of what God could do through our lives. Saul also had a problem with being insecure. Like a leaf tossed about the wind, Saul vacillated between feelings and convictions. Everything he said and did was selfish because he lived for himself. For example, Saul said his family was" the least" in the" smallest "tribe in Israel, which was Benjamin but 1 Samuel 9: 1 says his father was" a mighty man of power." Saul is not thankful for where he came from and what his family had accomplished. Saul didn't want to face the responsibility God had given him, in another situation Saul kept some war booty, which was things confiscated from warring with other nations , that shouldn't have been kept and then tried to blame his soldiers, he had no integrity ,and willing to lie to save face. , he then claimed that his soldiers had really taken it to sacrifice to God. God sees everything and he looks at the heart and remember in God's eyes obedience is better than sacrifice, so he was only fooling himself with the cover up.

Though Saul was called by God and had a mission in life, Saul struggled constantly with jealousy, insecurity, arrogance, impulsiveness, and deceit. He did not decide wholeheartedly to commit to God. Because Saul would not let God's love give rest to his heart, he never became God's man. This is true for a lot of us who are called by God to do His will. It probably will not to be king over a nation but whatever it is, we must take heart in wanting to obey God's will and do the right things. We may look good on the outside, and be pretending, taking shortcuts, being deceitful, lying, and not relying on God to help us, when we know we are falling out of God's will. When we feel weak and get caught up in the worldly things that prohibit us from doing God's will we need to go to God and confess our sins and the wrongs we have done and humble ourselves and he will forgive us and our relationship will be made right with God and we can move on to do God's work as He has purpose us. As a result of Saul's negligence to be obedient God and his impulsiveness that he even attempted to murder a young man named David that he had befriended and then became jealous of all his accomplishment, and he envied how famous he was becoming and spent many years try trying to hunt him down and kill him. We will learn of David and his relationship later in the story. Saul actually really lost his mind; he became so intent with this envy and jealousy that evil spirits took over his soul and mind he could no longer think as a man of God.

What was this evil spirit the Lord sent? Perhaps Saul was simply depressed. Or the Holy Spirit had left Saul and God allowed an evil spirit(demon) to torment him as judgement for his disobedience (this would demonstrate God's power over the spiritual world-1 Kings 22: 19-23). Either way Saul was driven to insanity, which led him to attempt to murder David.

"And Samuel said, Hath the Lord as great delight in burnt offerings and sacrifices, as in obeying the voice of the Lord? Behold, to obey is better than sacrifice, and to hearken than the fat of rams. For rebellion is the sin of witchcraft, and stubbornness is iniquity and idolatry. Because thou hast rejected the word of the Lord, he has also rejected thee from being king. (1 Samuel 15-22, 23).

David was anointed king, but it was done in secret; he was not publicly anointed until much later (2 Samuel 2:4; 5:3). Saul was still legally king, but God was preparing David, a mere shepherd boy for his future responsibilities. The anointing oil poured over David 'd head stood for holiness. It was used to set people or objects apart for God's service. Each king and High Priest of Israel was anointed with oil. This commissioned him as God's representative to the nation. Although God rejected Saul's' kingship by not allowing any of his descendants to sit on Israel's throne. Saul himself remained on the throne until his death.

When we think of David, we think shepherd, poet, giant- killer, king, ancestor of Jesus- in short, one of the greatest men in the Old Testament. But alongside that list stands another: betrayal, liar, adulterer, murderer. The first list gives qualities we all might like to have; the second qualities that might be true of any of us. The Bible makes no effort to hide David's failures. Yet he is remembered and respected for his heart for God. Knowing how much more we share in David's failure than his greatness, we should be curious to find out what made God refer to David as 'as a man after His own heart."

David, more than anything else, had an unchangeable belief in the faithful and forgiving nature of God. He was a man who lived with great zest. He sinned many times but was quick to confess his sins. His confessions were from the heart, and his repentance was genuine. David never took God's forgiveness lightly or his blessings for granted. In return, God never held back from David either His forgiveness or the consequences of his actions. David experienced the joy of forgiveness even when he had to suffer the consequences of his sins.

We tend to get these reversed. Too often we would rather avoid the consequences than experience forgiveness. Another significant difference between us and David is that while he sinned greatly, he did not send repeatedly. He learned from his mistakes because he accepted the suffering they brought. Often, we do not seem to learn from our mistakes or the consequences that result from those mistakes.

God fearing people like David and Samuel were used by God to lead nations, but they nevertheless had problems in family relationships.

God-fearing leaders cannot take for granted the spiritual well-being of their children. They are used to having others follow their orders, but they cannot expect their children to manufacture faith upon request. Moral and spiritual character takes years to build, and it requires continual attention and patient discipline. David served God well as king, but as a parent he often failed God and his children. Do not let your service to God, even in leadership positions take away so much of your time and energy that you neglect your other God-given responsibilities.

David's unborn son died in fulfillment of God's punishment for David and Bath-Sheba's adultery. Amnon, David's firstborn, raped Tamar, his half-sister and was later murdered by his, third son, Absalom in revenge for raping Tamar. Later he returned only to rebel against David. He set up a tent on his roof and slept with ten of David's wives there. His pride led to his death. Adonijah, fourth son, was very handsome, but it was recorded that he was never disciplined. He set himself up as king before David's death. His plot was exposed, and David spared his life, but his half-brother Solomon later had him executed. Solomon became the next king of Israel. Ironically, Solomon 's many wives caused his downfall.

A Conundrum in the Family
Epilogue

I've always had an innate interest in the study of behavior—what we now call psychology. In high school, I took my first psychology class, and it gave a name to the curiosity I'd always had about human behavior. I went on to attend North Carolina Central University in Durham, North Carolina, where I chose psychology as my major and sociology as my minor. I wanted to understand how and why people's lives intertwine with one another.

Though I didn't complete my degree or graduate as I had planned, my passion for learning about people never faded. I continued to read anything I could find on the subject and would watch documentaries to deepen my understanding of human nature. I was especially drawn to psychological thrillers and movies that explored how people's behaviors and mindsets change due to life events or circumstances. I often found myself observing people, wondering what the driving force was behind their actions and reactions.

Years later, after I became a born-again Christian, I came to realize the true source of human behavior. Through the Bible, I learned that we were conceived in sin and shaped in iniquity. We live in a world with both good and evil forces at play. We were created by a supernatural God who gave us free will—the ability to choose to follow Him or fall into temptation. The father of all lies, Satan, tries to pull us away from God, tempting us with paths of destruction.

While I had explored some of these concepts through the lens of psychology, I found that the Bible provided all the answers. The Word of God showed me how and why our biblical heroes and heroines often fell short in their relationships—they failed to heed God's commands. Men and women, inspired by the Holy Spirit, were sent to teach and guide people to follow God's will. Yet, when they strayed and didn't repent, they faced consequences. But through the sacrifice of Jesus Christ—God's only Son, who came to Earth and gave His life for us—we are all given a chance to live in eternity with Him.

God used prophets, judges, and leaders to guide His people. Even though many failed and were flawed, God's love always provided a way out. His grace is sufficient, and through His love, we are all given second chances to remain in a right relationship with Him. I want you to understand that perfection is not required, but repentance and faith in Christ allow us to find forgiveness. No matter what we go through, God is able and will always be with us, just as He was with the saints in the Bible.

We are all saints and sinners in this modern world. The struggles we face are not unlike those faced by the people in the Bible. As you read through these stories, I hope you see how God worked through their lives and how He can do the same for us. This book draws from the Bible, commentaries, and sources like *Psychology Today* to provide a deeper understanding of human behavior from a Christian perspective. I hope it inspires you to live in obedience to God and avoid the pitfalls of envy, jealousy, and strife—the destructive forces that Satan uses to attack us.

The spiritual world is real, and we must be diligent in prayer and watchfulness. As we live our lives trying to do the right thing and remain humble, we will find peace, healthy relationships, and success. You might even become a hero of the faith, like David, a man after God's own heart.

Jealousy, envy, and strife have no place in our families. God will work things out according to His plan, and if we trust in Him, we may avoid unnecessary suffering. Let God be our guide. And remember, the sins of the parents often ripple through to their children, amplified across generations.

Take heed of these lessons, and may God lead you to a life of peace and restoration.

Made in the USA
Columbia, SC
24 February 2025

54264182R10022